Comments

I love it. I work with business clients who have a tendency to over complicate and intellectualize the simplicity of the Principles. While this book will certainly serve as a wonderful introduction for their children, it may also help them have insights for themselves. There's a beautiful innocence and hope in seeing our thoughts as neutral bubbles that will disappear. That's a message for everyone.

— Cheryl Bond – Essential Resilience,
Executive Coaching and Business Consulting.

I have taught this understanding to many hundreds of adults, and when they see how much it reduces their psychological suffering and adds to their quality of life, they almost always say: 'why aren't children learning about this?' Sheena Oxer's story is a lovely and enjoyable way to help children catch on to the magic secret behind their experience, and likely save themselves a lot of the unnecessary anxiety and stress that so many people experience in life.

— Annika Hurwitt, Ph.D

As an author, teacher and therapist I often get requests from my students and clients for something to share with their young children. "If I only knew this when I was growing up!" is a refrain I hear often. Well, here it is in this early childhood gem on the Three Principles. It will be wonderful to now have something to share with parents. Just yesterday a young mom of four kids asked if there was anything she could give her children. I am so grateful I now can send this to her and all future requests.

— Joseph Bailey, Licensed Psychologist, Author, and Counsellor

This simple book has the potential to eradicate the complexities, issues and problems that naturally occur when we don't know where our experience is coming from. It offers a profoundly practical understanding that I feel is the future of the education system and indeed human evolution. What a wonderfully helpful resource for children – our future.

— Rudi Kennard, International Speaker-www.innateevolution.com

I work with business leaders many of whom happen to be parents. They often ask me to recommend books for their kids. I can't wait to recommend this one! The simplicity of Sheena's message and her illustrations really hit home. I expect the book to be read again and again planting a valuable life lesson in kids of all ages.

— Sandy Krot - Director of Learning at Insight Principles and co-author of Invisible Power: Insight Principles at Work

Countless books have been written about the underpinning of the imagination to the world we inhabit. Being and Time of Heidegger has 590 pages and Being and Nothingness of Sartre has 638 pages (to name but two). But nothing has been written so childishly simply in our choice of world view as Understanding Thoughts and Feelings. In this book we are relieved to find that we all knew about a happier way of being already and so do not have to read through the history of philosophy (phew!) We do not have to think and see our thoughts as something outside ourselves talking about a world outside that. We can live with all of our being the nothingness and time of the moment. I recommend Understanding Thoughts and Feelings 'A Walk to Grandpa's' by Sheena Oxer (16 pages including illustrations) as a guide for all ages and backgrounds!

— Philip Franses, Senior Lecturer Schumacher College, Director Global Synapses

This book is dedicated to my teachers,
who taught me to look insightfully within.
Especially Ann Ross, Dr Keith Blevens, Valda Monroe,
the teachings of Sydney Banks, and most of all
my wonderful family who teach me daily.

In the hope that this book will help to bring
greater harmony to children and families.

It is based on true events.

First Published 2019 by Sheena Oxer Publishing

A CIP catalogue record for this book is available from the British Library.

978-1-9161183-0-0

A tale of two stories

A walk to Grandpa's

By

Sheena Oxer

Story One

It is a lovely fresh spring day and Anna and her family decide to go for a walk to see her grandfather.

It isn't a long walk and Anna normally enjoys it. There is usually frothy milk and biscuits when she gets there.

The road they walk on takes them past a playground where Anna's best friend is playing with another girl.

Anna is immediately upset.

She is annoyed that her best friend should be there with someone else.
She is upset that she hasn't been asked to play.
She is angry that they might be talking about her.

She feels that they have deliberately left her out and are saying how much they like each other.
But worst of all, she wonders if her best friend doesn't like her any more and that's why she didn't ask her to go to the park.

By the time she arrives at her grandfather's, Anna is very upset and very cross with everyone.
She snaps at her little brother who wants to play.

She grumpily takes the frothy milk from Grandpa who is being his usual chirpy self. The biscuit isn't enough.

She is rude to her mother who says no to another biscuit.

She wants to leave and go home.

Story Two

It is a lovely fresh spring day and Anna and her family decide to go for a walk to see her grandfather.

It isn't a long walk and Anna normally enjoys it. There is usually frothy milk and biscuits when she gets there.

The road they walk on takes them past a playground where Anna's best friend is playing with another girl.

Anna feels immediately upset.

Then Anna remembers something, something that changes her view of things.

She remembers that when she is feeling upset, she is having an upset thought.

That the feeling she is having is always coming from a thought she is having.

She remembers that this is true about her feelings now.

She feels her feelings change and she has a smile about it to herself. She feels relaxed.

She walks on to Grandpa's feeling free and happy. When she arrives there, she asks her little brother to do a jigsaw with her.

She thanks Grandpa for the frothy milk he always makes for her, and enjoys it.
The biscuit is delicious too.

She asks for another biscuit and when her mother says no, she remembers that it is close to lunchtime.

She is peaceful and leans against her mum who puts her arm round her.

So, what was so different about the two stories?

In the first story, Anna feels very upset about seeing her friend playing with another girl. She doesn't realise that it is a thought that is creating that feeling and she gets more and more upset as she believes that her feelings are coming from her friend.

In the second story, Anna remembers that her feelings are coming from thought. Just by remembering that, she can see her thoughts more clearly. She knows that her feelings are not coming from her friend but from her thoughts about her friend. She immediately feels peaceful.

Thoughts are like bubbles, they come and they go.

Bubbles last a very short time.
Bubbles pop very quickly.

We don't have good bubbles and bad bubbles. They are just bubbles. Thoughts are the same. Thoughts last a very short time and they go very quickly.

A thought always comes with a feeling.
A feeling always comes with a thought.
This can only ever happen right now. In this moment.

When we are feeling happy, we are having happy thoughts. When we are feeling sad, we are having sad thoughts. Thoughts and feelings always happen together. They are like two sides of the same coin.

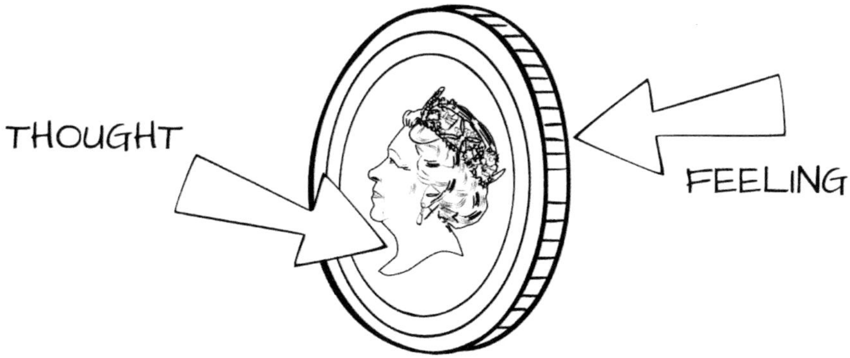

Understanding the logic of life

If I am thinking that I am feeling upset or happy because of what someone did to me, or for me, I am forgetting thought.

The logic is:
Feeling coming together with thought gives me the experience of life right now.

But if I believe that:
Feeling, and what someone did to me, gives me my experience, then I have forgotten thought. I am not understanding the logic.

If I understand that it is thought that makes me feel, then I understand that people can't make me feel sad or happy. It is only thought that can do this.

We don't need to change our thoughts, they change all the time on their own. Simply noticing it's thought is enough.

- THE END -

For adults reading this book

This book tells two stories based on the same set of circumstances, but each has a different ending.

The first story is based on the belief that people, circumstances and places have a direct and unavoidable impact on how we feel. Does that sound familiar to you? It's what most of us believe, and current psychology will tell you that it's true. This is an innocent misunderstanding that can lead to a great deal of unhappiness in all of us, and tension between us and our children.

We often hear statements like, "The school drop-off makes me feel so anxious" or, "You make me feel so cross when you are rude to me". But what if the school run, or somebody else's rudeness, isn't what's making us feel anxious or cross? What if those feelings actually only come from the fact that we are thinking about our experiences and judging them?

So how do we change that? Well, the good news is we don't have to. We don't have to change our thoughts or our child's thoughts because we are each gifted with our own powerful internal operating system, which is already working beautifully.

Sometimes we decide that some experiences are right and some experiences are wrong, but what if YOU are always OK. It's OK to feel whatever you feel. And that leads us to the second version of the story… The second story is based on a logical understanding of how our minds work. This logic shines a light on any misinterpretation of how we assume we operate. It's always been there. It comes to us in the moment, between the things that happen in life that are beyond our control, and our response to those things. It may look like we are responding to an event or to a person or to others' behaviour, but if we know that we cannot have a feeling without the corresponding thought (i.e. I can only feel anger when I have an angry thought; I can only feel happy when I have a cluster of happy thoughts), we begin to understand and see clearly that any reaction comes from our own thoughts about other people or events.

We can only feel what we think. This is only possible in the moment. Right now.

Consider this: the way we feel about a particular situation on one day may be wildly different from how we feel about the same situation on another day. We can experience a child's behaviour as irritating and annoying in one instance, and in another we can experience the same behaviour more peacefully, and react less. The child's behaviour is the same but our thoughts, and therefore our feelings, have changed. How is it that we can see the same behaviour differently? We don't make this happen. Our mind can change, and does change all the time.

This does not mean that we allow children or adults to behave in ways that are inappropriate. What it does mean is that we know that our feelings about that behaviour are coming from thought. Educating children about the role of thought can help them to understand their own thoughts and feelings.

Our thoughts are simply that: thoughts. Our thoughts move through us very fast. When we see that thoughts create feelings, we don't need to try to change them. Thoughts change on their own, very quickly in fact. Can you recall what your last thought was? Do you know what your next thought is going to be about?

Our personal thoughts change but the 'energy of Thought' does not; in other words the **fact** that we think does not change. We experience life via thought, it is a constant for us. When we bring together personal thought and the power of Thought into the singular, something amazing happens: judgement and self-blame falls away.

Yes, thought changes and can change back, so we are not seeking to change ourselves or to be different. However, by understanding the logic of how our minds are already working—that thoughts and feeling are coming together to create our experience of life—we can be much more aware that thoughts and feelings don't seem so compelling or true to us anymore. They are passing through us at great speed.

We come to understand this about ourselves in the same way as we understand gravity. We grow up seeing objects move downwards when we let go of them, then at some point we have a lesson about gravity, someone gives that movement a name and describes it to us. Gravity didn't just start, it has always been there. We can feel safe and secure in knowing that apples will not start floating upwards. In the same way we know that our feelings are always coming from thought right now and this comes with an absolute knowing and comfort that there is nowhere else to look. What I am describing here is that we are part of the system that has always been there.

The outcome of this new understanding is that we feel more peaceful, loving, and more connected, regardless of what we are thinking. This naturally gives us greater harmony in family life.

About the Author

Sheena Oxer

Sheena Oxer lives in Devon with her husband and their two children. She enjoys her allotment, nature, the outdoors, spending time with friends, going on dates with her husband, and being among her extended family. She also loves being an active part of her children's school.

Having studied Applied Biology at the University of Hertfordshire, Sheena went on to work in genetics research in the pharmaceutical industry. Following a move to Devon, she took up a research coordination position at the University of Exeter's Medical School. After a break from research to raise two young children to school age, Sheena retrained and now educates people in an understanding of how we experience life as human beings, working one-to-one or in groups, either on-line or in person. The word educate comes from the Latin *educaris*, which means to draw out (from within).

Sheena is passionate about mental well-being for everyone. She has long searched for a better way to make sense of her life, investigating many different approaches. That search ended when she came across this description of how we experience life. She has seen for herself, and through the experiences of her clients, just how powerful and incredibly beneficial it is to understand the relationship between thought and feeling. There is a logic to life. This understanding was first described by Sydney Banks. Later, Valda Monroe and Keith Blevens PhD (a clinical psychologist) recognised this as a paradigm shift—a change from how we thought we worked, to how we actually work.

This knowledge of how we experience life comes from within as an insight. Children see it to be true so quickly because they have had less time to copy us in our innocent misunderstanding of how we work.

Sheena educates her own children with this logic, and they love knowing this about themselves. Her family now comfortably live with their perfectly imperfect lives.

If we understand how we work as human beings, and how our experience is being created, then life can become so much easier. Sheena's wish for humanity is for greater harmony and less suffering.

Sheena is extremely grateful to have Ann Ross as a mentor, who shares this simplicity about life with such clarity. Ann always passes the credit on to The Priniciples at work.

www.sheenaoxer.co.uk